Stop Smoking

The Solitary Literary Work That Comprehensively Explores The Entirety Of Cessation Methodology, Rather

Than Narrowly Focusing On The Physiological Effects Of Nicotine Abstinence

Marijan Reinisch

TABLE OF CONTENT

Understanding The Implications Of Smoking....1

Identifying And Mitigating Factors That Can Lead To Smoking............17

What Is The Outcome When You Cease The Habit Of Smoking?............37

What Are The Available Resources And Support That Can Be Accessed?............49

Extinguishing The Flames: The Compelling Reasons To Cease This Act............68

Is Nicotine Replacement Therapy A Suitable Option For You?............107

Challenges............115

Avail Yourself Of All Available Assistance............129

In Order To Terminate One's Engagement, It Is Imperative To Contemplate This Matter Critically............144

Understanding The Implications Of Smoking

Include chapter material at this juncture...The cessation of smoking may emerge as a persistent component of your New Year's resolutions. Furthermore, some individuals even go as far as making it a heartfelt birthday aspiration. Nevertheless, these measures are insufficient if you genuinely aspire to cease the behavior in question.

Prudent consideration should be given to the adverse and deleterious consequences associated with the act of tobacco consumption. Are you aware that a solitary cigarette contains a minimum of seven thousand chemicals?

Two hundred and fifty of these chemicals have toxic properties, while seventy have a direct association with specific forms of cancer. Nevertheless, persistent research endeavors are being undertaken to ascertain the precise composition of the ingredients, specifically the undisclosed ones, by tobacco companies to both the general public and the US Food and Drugs Administration. It goes without saying that one should not be astonished by the discovery of novel chemicals present in cigarettes, as it remains an ongoing endeavor.

The substances and components present in cigarettes have been found to exert a significant impact on the human body.

Medical research has accumulated substantial evidence indicating that the chemicals present in cigarettes contribute to impaired organ function and a decline in the body's immune system. The health impacts of cigarette smoking are extensive and considerably alarming. This is rather astonishing considering that our acquaintances appear to refute the existence of these adverse consequences to such an extent that we are thoroughly persuaded that their smoking habit poses no issues.

In this chapter, it is anticipated that you will come to grasp the ramifications of smoking on the various facets of the human body. With a sense of consciousness and lofty aspirations, one will discover sufficient motivation to cease smoking within a span of 30 days.

Which naturally occurring ingredients present in cigarette smoke are considered toxic?

Prepare to be astonished by the substances you are currently inhaling. One inhalation consists of a combination of various chemical compounds. Once inhaled, the substance enters the respiratory system, where the lungs facilitate the transportation of the chemicals into the bloodstream. And could you please provide further clarification on the specific compounds classified as toxic?

The initial and most evident factor is the presence of nicotine. In less than ten seconds following inhalation, the nicotine swiftly reaches the smoker's brain. Upon prolonged usage of cigarettes, scientific studies indicate that nicotine is able to permeate all bodily systems, including the mammary glands, thereby potentially contaminating breast milk. This information is particularly relevant for nursing mothers.

Moving forward, carbon monoxide is the subsequent item on the roster. Carbon monoxide is found in the cigarette smoke. It typically induces the binding of the hemoglobin component to the red blood cells. Due to the presence of obstacles, the red blood cell's ability to function at its peak capacity and transport oxygen efficiently to various regions of the body is hindered. Due to diminished oxygen levels, the cells are unable to operate under normal conditions as well. In the event of severe circumstances, carbon monoxide poisoning may ensue.

An additional component comprises a cluster of substances known as carcinogens. This collective exhibits a significant range of diversity, as evidenced by the notable assortment of their compositions. These entities are grouped together under this overarching category due to their shared characteristic of causing the development of a sizable mass of irregular cells. They exhibit a high degree of reproductive activity and can give rise to malignancies. Cigarette smoking has been established as a direct cause of at least seventy documented cancers, and this figure continues to rise.

Furthermore, smoking can lead to the occurrence of oxidative stress. This could result in the modification of immune system functions. Additionally, it can result in DNA mutations that serve as precursors to cardiovascular diseases and the initial stages of cancer. Additionally, there exists a correlation between oxidative stress and the onset of premature aging. This issue can be addressed by adopting the supplementation of Vitamin E and other well-established antioxidants. Were you aware that, according to scientific examinations, individuals who do not smoke exhibit higher levels of antioxidants in their system? Moreover, the presence of oxidative stress can give rise to unmanageable inflammation, ultimately resulting in fatality.

To conclude, it may be unexpected to learn that cigarettes encompass high levels of heavy metals and radioactive substances. They are accompanied by tar, which is one of the challenging-to-eliminate constituents found in cigarette smoking. Over time, the detrimental impacts of these radioactive elements and heavy metals become apparent within the smoker's body.

Which illnesses are potentially associated with the habit of smoking?

Individuals who engage in smoking, as compared to those who do not partake in this habit, are exposed to a markedly elevated risk of mortality from various illnesses. As an illustration, were you aware that individuals who engage in smoking face a heightened susceptibility, ranging between two and four times, to succumb to coronary heart disease? The aforementioned statement holds true in the case of stroke as well. The risk of developing lung cancer is amplified by a factor of twenty-three for male individuals who smoke. Conversely, the risk of developing lung cancer is elevated by a factor of thirteen among women who smoke. With regards to mortality associated with COPD, smokers are afflicted at a magnitude of twelve to thirteen times higher than that of non-smokers.

What other statistics would convince a smoker to quit?

Educators ought to make an effort to abstain from excessively embellishing. It may be prudent for them to address the issues of smoking and mortality.

In the United States alone, an estimated annual death toll of nearly 500,000 individuals is attributed to the consumption of cigarettes. In the event that one endeavors to represent the global population, it becomes evident that nearly five million individuals perish due to tobacco-related occurrences. If the current trajectory of smoking habits persists, there will be a projected increase of 60 percent by the year 2030.

Were you aware that a minimum of 33.33 percent of cancer-related fatalities could have been averted in the event of a complete eradication of smoking? When examining the specific case of lung cancer, it is worth noting that 90% of men and 80% of women diagnosed with lung cancer have acknowledged being habitual smokers. In contrast, an examination of chronic obstructive pulmonary disease (COPD) reveals that 90% of fatalities can be attributed to the consumption of tobacco products.

The cumulative fatalities resulting from acts of homicide, transmission of HIV/AIDS, instances of suicide, criminal acts of murder, substance abuse in the form of alcoholism and illegal drug consumption, and injuries arising from motor vehicle accidents, remain significantly lesser in number compared to the fatalities caused by tobacco use. The utilization of tobacco remains the primary contributing factor to preventable fatalities on a global scale. Therefore, one could argue that engaging in cigarette smoking amounts to self-destructive behavior leading to a gradual suicide.

6

Indian Gooseberry

I

ndian

Gooseberry is

Convenient to purchase with a highly pleasing flavor. An outstanding characteristic of the Indian Gooseberry is its notable abundance of vitamin C as well as its tangy flavor. The consumption of Indian Gooseberry significantly alters the flavor profile of smoking, rendering it highly disagreeable and arduous to indulge in, ultimately leading to the cessation of smoking. However, it is also contingent upon the resiliency of your cardiac muscles. If one were to opt for cigarettes over Indian Gooseberry, it is certain that their life shall be consumed by smoke until the arrival of their demise.

7

Clove tree (SyZagium aromaticum)

C

love

tree is

Among the various herbs, some possess distinctive essential oils. This particular aromatic extract possesses calming properties that contribute to the alleviation of nervousness. It contains phenolic compounds, which possess antioxidant properties, provide relief from cough, and aid in combating halitosis. When consuming the desiccated flowers of the clove tree, it can assist in diminishing the reliance on tobacco products.

Identifying And Mitigating Factors That Can Lead To Smoking

One of the primary initial actions to effectively develop a cessation strategy as a tobacco user is to comprehend how to cope with triggers, specifically the individuals, locations, or stimuli that induce a craving or desire to partake in smoking or tobacco consumption. Your cessation endeavor will be rendered less arduous if you possess the ability to identify the stimuli that prompt your desire to smoke and strategize in anticipation of effectively managing those situations. Individuals have varying motivations that prompt them to initiate the habit of smoking, however, a few commonly observed factors include:

Indulging in the consumption of alcoholic beverages, tea, or coffee.

Completing a meal

Driving

Feeling tense, apprehensive, worried, bored, or depressed

Engaged in labor or in the pursuit of gainful occupation.

Engaging in festivities or finding pleasure

The environments in which you engaged in the habit of smoking or chewing tobacco with the highest frequency, such as bars and social gatherings, along with moments of heightened stress or consumption of coffee, are likely to be the circumstances in which your desire to smoke or chew tobacco is most pronounced.

Identify the stimuli that activate your smoking urges and devise a strategy to effectively handle or surmount them without resorting to tobacco consumption.

Sustaining your abstinence from smoking becomes increasingly arduous in the presence of alcoholic beverages. Thus, endeavor to consume a reduced amount of alcohol during the initial stages of abstinence. In a parallel manner, if you habitually engage in the action of smoking when consuming coffee, I would recommend attempting a transition to the consumption of tea for a designated timeframe of a few weeks.

Discover alternative activities to engage in if you typically partake in smoking following a meal, such as engaging in dental hygiene routines, embarking on a leisurely walk, communicating with a friend via text, or indulging in chewing gum.

Do not cultivate the circumstances that may lead to a resurgence of smoking. Ensure that you have a pen and paper readily available to engage in the activity of writing, rather than smoking, if you have the habit of smoking when using the phone.

Additional Factors: The Impact of Passive Smoking in the Workplace

The increased likelihood of non-smokers' health declining significantly arises when they are subjected to second-hand smoke within their workplace. Individuals who have effectively ceased the habit of smoking are prone to experience an increase in productivity within their professional endeavors. Moreover, individuals who have ceased smoking display a lower frequency of work absences in comparison to their smoking counterparts. Furthermore, research carried out by the U.S. National Cancer Institute indicates that individuals employed in smoke-free work settings exhibit a marked reduction in tobacco consumption compared to those who have the freedom to smoke while on the job. In conclusion, this study additionally demonstrated that individuals who smoke and aspire to quit are considerably more likely to succeed in their efforts if smoking is strictly prohibited in their workplace.

Why Quit Smoking?

There exist various factors that substantiate why it is advisable for you to cease the habit of smoking. These rationales extend beyond the scope of individual well-being to encompass the health of both oneself and others.

Cease the Habit of Smoking to Enhance Your Financial Savings

To begin with, smoking entails substantial financial costs. This is a direct consequence of the escalating prices of cigarettes and related products such as tobacco, paper, and filters, which continue to rise steadily due to the persistent implementation of tax hikes by legislators. This is due to the legislators' intent to dissuade individuals from engaging in smoking. Moreover, the expenditure incurred by individuals for healthcare services resulting from smoking-related illnesses is also significantly expensive. Hence, upon cessation of smoking, one would be able to accrue substantial financial savings – in certain instances, individuals who forgo smoking may even realize sufficient funds to cover a month's worth of rent on a recurring basis.

Additionally, employers are increasingly providing additional incentives to employees who choose to cease smoking. These incentives encompass the provision of gift cards or even monetary compensation. This will also serve to enhance the accumulation of your financial assets.

Cease the habit of smoking and evade feelings of frustration

As a result of the growing trend among cities and states to prohibit smoking in all public areas, the act of smoking has become increasingly inconvenient. It is probable that you will increasingly face the necessity of leaving the premises frequently to engage in smoking, or enduring detrimental weather conditions outdoors while indulging in smoking. These circumstances are far from favorable, and being exposed to the inclement weather while smoking could potentially result in an adverse impact on one's health.

Improve Your Senses

Strangely enough, smoking adversely affects one's sense of taste. Hence, should you choose to cease smoking, you will experience an enhancement in the gustatory perception of your meals. Additionally, your olfactory abilities will also see a noticeable amelioration. As a result, through renouncing smoking, one will be afforded the pleasure of experiencing previously unattainable joys, such as the delicate fragrance of roses.

By abstaining from the habit of smoking, you will acquire supplementary health advantages that have not been previously addressed.

Improve Your Sleep

It is common for individuals who indulge in smoking to experience fatigue even following a sufficient duration of sleep. This is due to the fact that, for evident reasons, they refrain from smoking during their slumber. As a result, they experience nicotine withdrawal throughout the nocturnal period. This results in their sleep being disturbed. Naturally, your physique will require a period of adaptation to the absence of smoking subsequent to your cessation. Nevertheless, you will soon experience cessation of nicotine withdrawal symptoms. Therefore, you will experience improved sleep.

Reinforce Your Bones

Ensuring optimal mineral density in your bones is crucial, as it signifies a robust skeletal structure. Tobacco smoking negatively impacts bone mineral density. Therefore, through the act of smoking, you are diminishing the strength of your skeletal structure.

Prevent Hearing Loss

Research has evidenced that smokers are at a heightened risk of experiencing hearing impairment in comparison to individuals who do not engage in smoking. Consequently, by abstaining from smoking, you are mitigating the risk of experiencing hearing impairment.

Enhance Your Sexual Well-being through Smoking Cessation

Ceasing the habit of smoking enhances your sexual experience. This can be attributed to the effect of smoking on blood circulation. If there is an inadequate circulation of blood in the genital region, individuals, regardless of their gender, may encounter difficulties in attaining arousal.

Finally, it is imperative to consider that smoking does not solely revolve around oneself. It also concerns others. It is unjust to compromise the well-being of others due to one's craving for a cigarette. The aforementioned justifications should suffice to prompt individuals to overcome their nicotine dependence, thereby ceasing the habit of smoking permanently.

Essential Information to Be Acquainted with

Quitting smoking is difficult. Presented below are a range of strategies that have the potential to aid you in your endeavor to cease smoking.

Compose a comprehensive enumeration of the rationales driving your decision to resign and securely retain them in your possession. Describe them when tempted.

Establish a definitive cessation date while simultaneously discontinuing completely. Some individuals are inclined towards the concept of gradually reducing their consumption. Fortunately, research has demonstrated that individuals who reduce their cigarette consumption tend to compensate by smoking a greater quantity per cigarette, resulting in minimal variance in nicotine levels. Therefore, it is generally most advantageous to ultimately resign on a predetermined date.

Inform all individuals of your decision to terminate the habit of smoking. Typically, both friends and family provide assistance and support. The presence of smoking individuals within the household exacerbates the difficulty of relinquishing the habit. If feasible, endeavor to encourage other household members who engage in smoking, or acquaintances who are smokers, to simultaneously embark on a cessation journey. Collaboration could prove significantly more effortless in contrast to taking on the task individually.

Kindly dispose of ashtrays, lighters, and cease the presence of all cigarettes.

Await some drawback symptoms. Upon cessation of smoking, individuals may experience various symptoms encompassing nausea, headaches, anxiety, irritability, cravings, and an overall sense of discomfort. The presence of these symptoms can be attributed to the cessation of nicotine, to which your body has become accustomed. Frequently, they attain their highest point approximately 12-24 hours later, subsequently diminishing gradually over a span of 2-4 weeks.

Prepare for a coughing. It is customary for individuals who quit smoking to experience a significant exacerbation in their coughing as their airways regain vitality. Many individuals assert that this exacerbates their condition in the aftermath of smoking cessation and reinforces their inclination to resume smoking. Please refrain from succumbing to this temptation. Typically, the cough gradually subsides.

Exercise caution in circumstances that may induce a desire to engage in smoking. More precisely, the consumption of alcohol is commonly linked to an inability to successfully quit smoking. It is imperative to consider limiting alcohol consumption during the initial weeks following smoking cessation. Consider modifying your daily regimen during the initial period of two to three weeks. By way of illustration, it would be prudent to abstain from visiting the club temporarily, especially if it serves as a tempting environment to indulge in both smoking and consuming alcoholic beverages. Likewise, if drinking tea and also coffee are tough times, try drinking generally fruit juice as well as a lot of water rather.

Take someday each time. Differentiate each day of success on a calendar. Please consider scrutinizing your actions when you experience a strong inclination to engage in smoking, and remind yourself firmly of your desire to avoid relapsing.

Declare. You may inform individuals of your non-smoking status. You will emit a more pleasant scent. Following a few weeks, it is expected that one's physical well-being will significantly improve, leading to heightened sensory perception of food and reduced frequency of coughing. You will experience an increase in your financial resources. Consider setting aside the funds that would typically be allocated for purchasing cigarettes, in order to indulge in enjoyable rewards.

Food. Certain individuals experience heightened concerns about weight gain following smoking cessation, as cravings may be exacerbated. Anticipate an increase in cravings, and make an effort to refrain from indulging in fatty or sugary substances as snacks. Consider opting for sugar-free gum and fruit as a viable alternative.

Do not succumb to despair in the event of coming up short. Analyze the justifications for your perception of heightened difficulty during that particular period. It will enhance your resilience and fortitude for future occasions. A considerable number of individuals who eventually cease the habit of smoking have undertaken three or four prior endeavors to do so.

What Is The Outcome When You Cease The Habit Of Smoking?

We are commencing the initiation of your smoking cessation program. Prior to proceeding with that particular stage, it is imperative that you garner a comprehensive understanding of the entire process. Understanding the physiological and neurological aspects occurring within your body will not only facilitate adherence to your goals, but also instill the impetus necessary to persistently strive towards achieving new milestones. Additionally, maintaining a record of the chronology of symptoms and achievements will provide reassurance that one is not enduring the journey in isolation, as countless individuals have encountered identical symptoms and overcome them to thrive as accomplished individuals who have successfully quit smoking. One of the strategies that will be elaborated upon in the subsequent chapters pertains to utilizing this timeline in order to acquire foresight, comprehending the forthcoming events and benefits that ensue as one embarks on the path of nicotine withdrawal and abstinence.

One hour subsequent to your cessation of cigarette consumption, there is a considerable reduction in your blood pressure.

4 Hours Following the Last Cigarette: Substantial manifestation of withdrawal symptoms ensues, as the body becomes

aware of the gradual decline in nicotine levels within the bloodstream, reaching their lowest levels in recent memory (or at least since the previous attempt to cease smoking).

Following an 8-hour interval from your last cigarette, you will notice an initial culmination of heightened anxiety levels. It is advisable to acclimate yourself to this anxiety and potentially establish a rapport with it, as it is anticipated to persist in varying manifestations for a significant duration of several days, at minimum. The normalization of anxiety levels and restoration of equilibrium may require a period of up to two weeks. Nevertheless, following a period of approximately 48 hours, the apprehension will become significantly more manageable.

Within a 24-hour period from your last cigarette, it is advisable to refrain from engaging in interpersonal interactions. If you are required to work, it is advisable to avoid direct involvement in customer service, as there is a heightened likelihood of encountering heightened levels of anger and irritability. One might experience unexplained anger and observe that even the slightest triggers provoke irritability. This trend will persist for the subsequent 24 hours, subsequently experiencing a gradual decline as you transition into the third day. Nevertheless, the 24 hour milestone carries significant advantages. It will be apparent to you that your lung capacity has already shown improvement after merely one day of abstaining from cigarettes, and this improvement will persistently grow as you continue to steer clear of smoking.

Upon the elapse of 48 hours since your last cigarette, the majority of physical and emotional symptoms shall culminate at their peak intensities. Upon reaching this point, one can anticipate a decline in symptoms and physical effects, rather than an increase in them. This does not imply that the cessation of withdrawal symptoms will be absolute. In fact, the period following the initial decline can be particularly perilous for individuals attempting to quit smoking, as they may underestimate the risk of relapse and become lured by the allure of cigarettes, testing to ascertain if they have indeed overcome their addiction. It is important to remain vigilant and not succumb to such ploys. This is just your body and mind trying anything, desperate for a dose of nicotine. Additionally, it can be observed that one's gustatory and olfactory perception undergoes enhancement within a span of 48 hours.

72 Hours Following the Cessation of Smoking: As aforementioned, the intensity of your cravings generally reaches its maximum by the 48th hour. However, in some instances, cravings may persist up to the third day. Nevertheless, following a period of 72 hours, individuals generally experience cigarette cravings a mere 3-4 times daily. Continue to prepare yourself for the battle ahead, as while the frequency of cravings may be diminishing, their intensity may remain unchanged or even intensify. In fact, some of the cravings

encountered during this phase will be the most potent ones thus far. Regard these cravings as a viral infection that your body is actively combating; as this infection reaches its end, its desperation for nicotine intensifies. Don't give in. A notable improvement can be observed in your respiratory patterns, as you will observe a significant ease in your breathing. If one is inclined, they might be capable of ascending staircases without interruption, engaging in physical exertion with greater ease, or possibly experiencing enhancements in their vocal abilities, assuming they take pleasure in such an activity. Although complete restoration of your lung function will not be attained by the conclusion of the third day, a significant enhancement will be discernible.

Following a period of two weeks since your most recent cigarette, you will have successfully overcome your dependency. Your urges will decrease to a few occasions per week, and by the third week, they will have practically vanished entirely. Furthermore, a noticeable improvement in your dental well-being will be evident to you and your dear ones. As a consequence, you will notice a favorable enhancement in your breath's odor, along with a significant improvement in the health of your gums and a notable whitening effect on your teeth. This phenomenon is a result of the convergence of two aspects. Firstly, your body has an enhanced capacity to facilitate the utilization of vitamin C when you abstain from smoking, thereby enabling a greater amount of this nutrient to contribute to the preservation of gum and tooth health. Secondly, by ceasing smoking, you will prevent the accumulation of dental plaque on your teeth.

Upon reaching the four-week mark following cessation of smoking, your body will embark on a significant restoration process. As a result, your immune system will fortify, rendering you more resilient, and diminishing the likelihood of infections. As the cilia in your lungs undergo regeneration, they facilitate a more efficient clearance of mucus, thereby enhancing your lung function.

Three Months following Smoking Cessation: During this period, the physical changes may not be readily apparent; however, there is a significant reduction in the likelihood of experiencing a heart attack. Furthermore, as time progresses, the risk of developing lung cancer decreases by approximately 50%. In a span of 10-15 years, the probability of you developing lung cancer will be equivalent to that of an individual who has never engaged in smoking.

Prior to proceeding to the subsequent chapter, which initiates the commencement of your cessation endeavors, kindly cease reading momentarily and proceed to designate a specific date on the calendar to solemnly pledge your commitment to the act of quitting. It is imperative that you exercise caution when selecting the day of commencement, as initiating your endeavor during a week when your stress levels are already elevated could potentially result in unsuccessful cessation. It is essential to designate a timeframe during which you can dedicate the majority of your time and effort to the process of ceasing smoking, particularly within the initial three-day period, or ideally, extending up to the initial two weeks. Once you have selected a day, kindly return and peruse Chapter Five on the morning of your awakening. Refrain from smoking in the morning of your cessation. It has been suggested that commencing the day by having your final cigarette may facilitate the process of quitting. This is absolutely false. Having completed a duration of 8 hours of sleep, you have effectively progressed one-third of the way into your initial day of abstaining from smoking. It is imperative to consume your ultimate cigarette prior to retiring for the night and initiate your smoking cessation journey promptly on the subsequent day.

What Are The Available Resources And Support That Can Be Accessed?

An extensive array of tools encompassing social support, community resources, classes, and various other aids can serve as valuable resources and support mechanisms. This particular chapter encompasses a broader range of content than you might anticipate. Each and every individual can greatly benefit from assistance provided by external sources. There are various alternative courses to explore when seeking assistance.

First, let me explain. Isolation is terrible. I have sufficiently conveyed my message, but due to my inclination towards extensive discourse, I shall now provide further elaboration. Isolation and prolonged solitude may result in a proclivity towards relapse, as it fosters excessive self-reflection. It is worth noting that relapse refers to the act of reverting back to tobacco use or the consumption of other substances. The term "relapse mode" refers to a situation where an individual exhibits a confluence of behaviors that are likely to result in relapse. Isolation constitutes one of those behaviors. Indeed, it serves as one of the most notable factors in the decline, notwithstanding the individual's exemplary performance in all other spheres.

Reaching Out

Assistance and provisions can be instrumental in navigating and overcoming this situation, in addition to the literature discussed in the previous chapter. When we actively seek assistance from others to establish a support network, we can find solace in knowing that we do not face our difficulties in isolation, thereby mitigating the risk of social isolation. As human beings, we possess a fundamental inclination towards socialization, and the influence we derive from our interactions with others can bestow upon us greater fortitude and foster a sense of responsibility.

For individuals who tend to be solitary and are hesitant to seek assistance, initiating contact can be exceedingly challenging. One might inquire into the significance of this matter, as they perceive themselves to be distinct from the rest of the population. In this particular context, your distinction is notable, as it aligns with the general trend of similarities among the rest. I don't like people. It is quite ironic, considering that I engage in constant conversations with individuals throughout every moment of the day, both in the morning and at night; nevertheless, this statement holds true. I anticipate feeling apprehensive about attending work due to the necessity of engaging in interpersonal communication, as my social anxiety reinforces the inclination to withdraw from such interactions. However, I feel the power of people surrounding me. During the initial hour of my day, I metamorphose into a gregarious individual and experience a profound sense of satisfaction. That exemplifies the influence derived from the presence of individuals. It enables the development of a more resilient and improved iteration of oneself.

An alternative method to circumvent seclusion and regression would be to become a member of various associations, for instance: online discussion boards, support organizations dedicated to tackling underlying factors that perpetuate smoking, virtual communities on social media platforms like Facebook, professional counseling, and attendance at meetings organized by Nicotine Anonymous.

Forums

Do you harbor concerns about the potentially pervasive influence exerted by Facebook's dominant control over the minds of individuals? Try the old forums. They are instrumental in accessing knowledge and experiences that have proven effective for others. In this scenario, numerous individuals would recommend literary works and audiovisual resources that aided them in addressing their habit, and might seek insights from others regarding their experiences with overcoming the initial stage of abstinence. Check out the QuitNow message-boards.[4]

Facebook

In light of the fact that a significant number of individuals, excluding myself, currently reside on Facebook, it is evident that Facebook encompasses groups for various topics. I mean everything. There is little additional information to be provided regarding Facebook. If you have yet to experience it, I encourage you to give it a try. Try searching Facebook groups. You will be overwhelmed by the extensive array of tribes that you come across, causing a whirl of thoughts in your mind. Visit your Facebook profile or establish an account on the official Facebook website at facebook.com. On your personal Facebook page, locate the "Groups" option on the left side of the screen. In the search bar positioned at the top of the page, attempt to input the phrase "quitting smoking support." As a result, a substantial list of options will be displayed for your consideration. Choose any of them and experiment with a wide variety. Please refrain from becoming overly engrossed in extraneous or unnecessary matters. In the concluding chapter of this book, you will find a web address that can be readily copied and pasted in order to access a Quit Smoking Group expeditiously upon logging in.

NA- Emphasizing the Importance of a Personalized Approach

Nicotine Anonymous can prove beneficial with regards to fostering a sense of continuity and camaraderie within a physical collective. Individuals consistently offer their presence and organize regular gatherings, either on a weekly or bi-weekly basis, to maintain ongoing communication. The groups provide an opportunity for you to establish connections with like-minded individuals who share your commitment to cessation. They also offer the well-established and proven twelve-step program that has effectively assisted numerous individuals struggling with alcohol addiction within the Alcoholics Anonymous (AA) community. Under no circumstances should it be assumed that a twelve-step gathering dedicated to various substances - of which there are numerous - bears any resemblance to a religious institution or a manipulative group enforcing actions against one's will. You may simply participate in order to be in the company of those who may be facing challenges, and even extend assistance to others as you progress towards your own recovery. Therefore, I suggest giving the no smoking groups a try, perhaps even prior to making the decision to quit. You will be welcomed or granted admission to numerous meetings. You may inform them that you have refrained from smoking for a duration of ten minutes. Discover a gathering in any locality by accessing the website at https://nicotine-anonymous.org/ [6].

Pharmaceuticals as a Means of Assistance

I had initially contemplated excluding this form, but ultimately elected to include it to acknowledge the invaluable aid and contribution of medication. I have been made aware that certain individuals have obtained significant support by employing pharmaceutical treatments such as Wellbutrin and Chantix. I initially omitted this information due to the adverse effects I experienced from the medications. Notwithstanding, individuals vary in significant ways. If you have an interest, please consult with your healthcare professional to determine if these options may be suitable for your circumstances. I abandoned the pursuit of this approach as I had administered an ample amount of medications and had already achieved a satisfactory level of stability. Upon incorporating cessation medications, I experienced the unfavorable consequence of nausea during my attempts to utilize them.

Furthermore, should you choose to resort to drug utilization as a means of assistance, exercise extreme caution and remain mindful of their potential interactions with your brain chemistry.

Assisting Others and the Positive Emotions it Elicits

There remains one final point to address in this context. Engaging with others entails not only benefiting from their assistance, but also actively offering aid, which in turn can enhance one's own well-being. The depth of emotion experienced when individuals confide in you, regarding the impact of your words in igniting a fresh perspective that influenced their decision to reconsider, is truly indescribable. You will be highly acknowledged and your contribution to their achievement will leave you with a profound sense of fulfillment and impact on life. When you render assistance to others, you shall receive emotional gratification in return, should you desire it.

Summary

We can all derive advantages from receiving assistance when undertaking a significant transformation in our lives. Incorporating various modalities of support groups into your preparation regimen may constitute a crucial component that can propel you towards achieving success. If you are of the belief that you are self-sufficient and do not require assistance, I implore you to make a genuine attempt to acquire support. If one does not find satisfaction in social interactions and the assistance received fails to yield any benefits, it is permissible to articulate

tried. For the majority of individuals, the concept of "strength in numbers" holds true. Furthermore, should you have an interest in pursuing medication or seeking primary care assistance, it is highly recommended to explore these avenues. One can never have an excess of support in these matters.

TAKE A BREAK

Congratulations on your remarkable progress! Your initiative to thoroughly educate yourself before embarking on the journey of smoking cessation sets you apart from others. Nevertheless, it is advisable to introspect at this juncture.

As an avid reader, I am aware that I possess strong personal views when engaging with books, often leading me to struggle with aligning my perspectives with those presented by the author. Please do not be overly critical of me.

As uncertainties may already be arising in your mind, engaging in the practice of incorporating awareness checkpoints can be a valuable exercise should you proceed with your decision to quit, irrespective of any subpar information you have encountered thus far.

Try this exercise. Create a comprehensive inventory delineating the reasons for relinquishing the habit of smoking as opposed to the factors that may dissuade one from abandoning it. It is evident that there are no valid justifications listed in the "reasons against" category. Attempt to approach the situation by analyzing the reasons behind your decision to cease, juxtaposed with envisioning the concerns that may dissuade you from desisting. Self-perception can be quite elusive. The prevalence of individuals who engage in smoking activity is considerably greater than one might anticipate. It bestows upon us a comprehensive understanding of our identity. Nevertheless, our essence remains unchanged, regardless of the presence of a substance that is detrimental to our well-being. Are you prepared to discontinue the habit? Check yourself.

Compare your two lists. If you are genuinely committed to quitting smoking, your list of reasons should be more extensive. I apologize, but I do not imply that it needs to significantly surpass the other list in height or prominence. As long as there exists a numerical difference of at least one between the two, it is deemed favorable. The purpose is to assess your current situation and determine the level of your commitment towards cessation.

Conversely, if your list of reasons against it is more extensive, it is advisable to conduct further investigation. Be aware that embarking on the endeavor to cease a habit or activity may determine the course of your journey. You alone possess the ability to determine the extent of your motivation to cease. If your list of reasons against quitting is extensive, I would advise you to carefully evaluate the validity of those reasons in order to determine their reasonableness. In the majority of instances, when approached with rationality, the items included in the "why not" category typically lack substantial validity. Do not surrender if you perceive yourself inclining toward abstaining from cessation. Perhaps you can streamline it to a reduced number of justifiable reasons to remain. Moreover, you might even delve into the underlying reasons why you perceive the act of relinquishing control as detrimental. Make an effort to resolve those issues in order to proceed with the prominence of the "why" list over the other list.

Given that you have reached this stage, it is highly probable that your commitment is genuine, and you are determined to proceed further. That is excellent news! Additionally, I strongly encourage you to explore alternative strategies that can enable you to assess your level of motivation and dedication.

Furthermore, I advise revisiting the journal as previously mentioned. Engaging in the act of composing and carefully assessing your compositions can be advantageous in perceiving distinctions over time, thereby sustaining your drive and motivation.

Summary

Once more, I would like to convey to you that you possess remarkable abilities!

Even if you were to complete this entire book without wavering or hesitating, and should you choose to refrain from giving up or making attempts, persistently engaging with its content will greatly contribute to your accumulation of valuable knowledge for your future endeavors. Continue progressing by regularly evaluating your performance and maintaining a conscious awareness of the underlying motivation behind your actions. We shall proceed with additional recommendations in the subsequent chapters that could prove advantageous to you.

Extinguishing The Flames: The Compelling Reasons To Cease This Act

'The act of smoking poses significant risks to one's overall well-being.' It is possible that you have encountered, perused, or been exposed to this quote at some point. However, what is the underlying reason for its detrimental impact? What are the physiological effects of smoking on the human body? Additionally, how does the aforementioned factor influence the remaining facets of your life, including your financial state, familial relationships, and social connections?

Immediate Consequences of Smoking" or "Immediate Impact of Smoking

When an individual initiates smoking, observable immediate consequences ensue. Despite the abundant evidence of these adverse consequences, individuals continue to disregard them. Certain things are evident, while others quietly develop without one's awareness. These short-term effects include:

Elevated susceptibility to respiratory ailments such as upper respiratory tract infections and tuberculosis

Bad breath

Dental discoloration characterized by yellowing

Unpleasant odor emitted by garments and locks

Bad taste in mouth

Gum disease

Elevated heart rate

Recurring cough and bronchitis

Increased incidence of asthma

Respiratory system impairment

Prevalence of skin aging at an early stage

Damage to the respiratory system can have immediate detrimental consequences that may eventually evolve into the underlying cause of chronic diseases. Insufficient pulmonary function results in dyspnea and a persistent cough. Moreover, due to compromised pulmonary function, individuals who smoke often experience fatigue when engaged in cardiovascular and other strenuous exercises.

The Long-Term Consequences of Smoking

One of the primary factors contributing to the cessation of smoking among the majority of individuals is apprehension surrounding their health. This is undeniably a significant and pressing issue: given that the multitude of chemicals, exceeding 4,000 in number, present in tobacco pose significant health risks, as they permeate the entire body and have adverse effects on every organ within our physiology. Indeed, approximately 50% of individuals within the smoking demographic would ultimately succumb to an ailment directly caused by their tobacco consumption.

Heart Diseases and Stroke

Individuals who engage in smoking activities face a twofold increase in the likelihood of succumbing to heart attacks compared to those who do not partake in smoking.

Smoking constitutes a prominent contributor to the development of cardiovascular disease, precipitating a constriction of blood vessels in the extremities. Men who smoke are also susceptible to experiencing erectile dysfunction as a result of vascular disease.

- Additionally, the blood vessels, particularly those responsible for supplying blood to the brain, undergo impacts. The obstruction they experience has the potential to result in a cerebrovascular accident.

- While it is indeed factual that smoking is a major contributor to the development of

lung cancer, along with numerous other types of cancer, statistical data reveals that a larger portion of mortality associated with smoking stems from fatalities resulting from cardiovascular conditions such as heart diseases and stroke.

- Each year, approximately 181,000 individuals in the United States succumb to heart diseases and stroke caused by smoking, whereas 158,000 individuals die from smoking-related cancer.

Lung diseases

As the smoker persists in their habit, their lungs endure concomitant and substantial harm.

- Emphysema is characterized by a decline in the elasticity of the bronchioles,

which are the small airways connecting the alveoli in the lungs. If one's capacity to expand their lungs is impaired, it results in an inability to exhale completely and disrupts the equilibrium of chemicals in the bloodstream.

- Chronic Bronchitis: The respiratory passages undergo structural alterations, leading to impairment of the mucus-producing glands. The enlargement of the mucus glands results in persistent coughing and the production of sputum.

- Chronic Obstructive Pulmonary Disease, commonly referred to as COPD, encompasses a range of respiratory conditions which significantly impede an individual's ability to breathe. It exacerbates progressively and may ultimately result in mortality.

Cancers

- Many individuals have an understanding that smoking is associated with the development of lung cancer, yet not everyone is cognizant of the fact that this habit also escalates the risk of acquiring cancer in the following areas:

Upper respiratory tract

Mouth

Nose

Larynx

Throat

Esophagus

Liver

Stomach

Pancreas

Kidney

Bladder

Ovary

Cervix

Colon

Rectum

Blindness

- Smoking elevates an individual's susceptibility to macular degeneration. Macular degeneration may result in the development of cataracts, a condition characterized by the opacity of the ocular lens.

Potential dangers to expectant mothers and infants

- Women who smoke have a higher risk of having an ectopic pregnancy. Additionally, they possess an elevated susceptibility to experiencing a miscarriage or delivering an infant with a low birth weight.

- Infants with a low birth weight are at greater risk of mortality or may experience cognitive or physical impairments upon birth.

- Expectant mothers who engage in smoking are at an increased risk of giving birth to infants with physical deformities such as cleft lip and cleft palate.

Approximately 480,000 fatalities in the United States are ascribed to smoking annually, representing a ratio of 1 in 5 deaths. Furthermore, according to the Centers for Disease Control and

Prevention (CDC), it has been estimated that male smokers experience a reduction of approximately 13.2 years in life expectancy, while female smok

The Advantages of Smoking Cessation: Progressive Health Benefits Associated with Quitting Smoking

Regardless of whether you fall into the category of a novice teenage smoker, an avid and frequent smoker, or lie somewhere in the middle, the present moment presents an opportune occasion to cease the act of smoking. The advantages of ceasing smoking would manifest themselves nearly immediately and invariably result in an improved state of well-being and increased longevity.

Individuals who voluntarily abstain from smoking will experience an increased overall lifespan compared to those who persist in their smoking habits. Health issues, particularly those pertaining to the respiratory system, also undergo cessation. These advantages are inclusive of individuals of both genders, spanning all age groups, and encompassing even those who have been diagnosed with diseases caused by smoking.

"Chronological Presentation of the Advantages of Smoking Cessation:

Following a cessation period of 20 minutes, your heart rate will have returned to a normal state.

After a period of 12 hours since cessation – The carbon monoxide concentration in your bloodstream will have returned to its baseline level. At elevated concentrations, carbon monoxide poses a potential toxicity to the human body.

After a span of 24 hours since cessation, it is remarkable to note that the previously heightened risk of heart attack by 70% for individuals who smoke would commence a gradual decline. For a single day's duration, you have not yet completely resolved your difficulties, however, you have certainly made significant progress.

Within a period of approximately two to three weeks following cessation, individuals can expect their pulmonary capacity to experience marked enhancement, allowing for increased engagement in physical endeavors without the sensation of respiratory distress. You will begin to experience improved respiration. Phew! What a relief!

Within a period of 1 to 9 months following cessation, the restorative process of your lungs will commence. The cilia within your lungs will restore their capacity to regulate mucus production and facilitate lung cleansing. The likelihood of developing respiratory infections will significantly decrease.

One year post cessation, the likelihood of experiencing a heart attack is reduced by 50%.

After a period of five years following cessation, the likelihood of developing upper respiratory cancers and bladder cancer is reduced by fifty percent. The risk of developing cervical cancer and stroke returns to that of an individual who does not smoke.

After a decade of cessation, the likelihood of developing lung cancer is decreased by 50%.

Following a cessation period of fifteen years, the probability of experiencing a heart attack is restored to the level comparable to that of an individual who has never smoked.

The Impacts of Smoking on Various Dimensions of your Life

Budget

In addition to the objective of improving one's overall health, ceasing tobacco consumption also posits various supplementary advantages. Let's face it. Tobacco products are not naturally occurring and they are not provided without cost. You are expending finances on each individual cigarette. If an individual habitually ignites a carton containing 20 cigarettes per day, the resultant consumption amounts to 7,300 *cigarettes on a yearly basis. Even with the selection of the most affordable brand, an approximate expenditure of $2,000 per year can be expected. In addition to the financial burdens associated with the potential illnesses, it has a profound impact on your budget.*

In order to gain a more comprehensive understanding of the financial implications of smoking, calculate the annual expenditure on cigarettes by multiplying the daily expense by 365. Subsequently, calculate the product of this value and the duration in years during which you have engaged in the act of smoking. Is it shocking? Consider all of the alternative activities you could engage in with such a substantial sum of money.

Social Circle and Acceptance

Generally, smoking is not that socially acceptable today. In corporate settings, there exists a designated area allocated for individuals who engage in smoking activities, and certain employers exhibit a preference for prospective employees who do not partake in tobacco consumption. Upon reflection, it can be discerned that employees who engage in smoking are prone to experiencing illness, thus resulting in a correlative rise in instances of absenteeism and sick leave.

Smoking is prohibited in public environments, including educational institutions, governmental establishments, dining establishments, social gatherings, and similar locations. In the process of leasing residential units, property owners tend to have a preference for tenants who do not engage in smoking, as this demographic possesses reduced maintenance expenses and poses a lower fire hazard. In social contexts, it is not uncommon for acquaintances to kindly request refraining from smoking inside their homes or vehicles.

Health of Other People

It is possible that you are familiar with the term 'secondhand smoking', which is also referred to as environmental tobacco smoke. When individuals who abstain from smoking are exposed to the smoke emanating from the burning tip of a cigarette or the smoke expelled by a smoker, they inadvertently inhale not only nicotine but also other deleterious chemicals. It can be likened to passive exposure to secondhand smoke. Even when individuals in your proximity refrain from smoking, sharing space with them while engaging in smoking activities poses a potential threat to their lives as well. They are exposed to the identical harmful substances as yourself. One might hold the belief that smoking solely poses a threat to one's own life, however, it is important to recognize that smoking has detrimental effects on those in close proximity as well.

React

Consider the case of the adolescent who, during their college years, partook in a singular instance of cigarette experimentation at a social gathering. Subsequent to this encounter, the individual experienced an overwhelming aversion, accompanied by distressing bouts of coughing, prompting an immediate renunciation of the habit, thereby ensuring a lifelong abstinence from smoking. Did she/he perish as a result of inhaling that solitary puff? Do we not each hold comparable recollections of such youthful escapades? What about the middle-aged individual who commenced smoking in response to societal pressures, feelings of insecurity, stress, or lifestyle modifications, as well as their struggle to find personal identity, but subsequently abandoned this habit when their circumstances evolved or when influenced by moral beliefs? What criteria do you use to differentiate between a personal desire to discontinue and a genuine necessity to terminate one's involvement? One has the ability to guide a horse to the river, but coercion will not compel it to drink. Your mental state, circumstances, and perspective may have culminated to this particular juncture. Once you have made your decision, kindly note that this is my final cigarette, and I expect you to uphold your commitment. However, it is worth mentioning that there is no such concept as "the final cigarette" if one genuinely intends to quit. The preceding stick was the one which you consumed for smoking purposes on the previous day. Once you have firmly resolved to cease smoking, you have renounced all visual, tactile, gustatory, and indeed all connections with cigarettes. Detach yourself from stimuli that may induce adverse reactions.... The various aspects of your environment, social network, and familiar surroundings that elicit associations with a cigarette

Please ascertain the indicators that trigger your desire to engage in smoking. Cessation of smoking presents a greater psychological hurdle than a physical one. Every action elicits an equal and opposite reaction... During the course of nicotine withdrawal, individuals frequently experience feelings of emptiness, irritability, and restlessness, accompanied by sporadic waves of unpredictable emotions and unwarranted assumptions. It is advisable to expect that the circumstances of abstaining from it may vary. Prepare in advance and execute swiftly. Procure an item or substance to alleviate the emptiness. Do not limit yourself to a single activity; instead, engage in a variety of pursuits to completely divert your interest away from cigarettes.

Create a buffer activity.. Engage in alternative activities when the cravings arise..

Get ready... The urges are bound to arise at any given moment.

Kill it off. The cultivation of a robust determination to resist the temptation of smoking is not overly challenging to acquire. Remember to tell yourself. I will not perish if I refrain from smoking promptly.

Seek assistance and backing. Convey your intention to cease smoking to someone whom you are acquainted with, and who possesses the ability to motivate and support you in implementing this behavioural alteration. It is possible that the person who has an impact on you or whom you hold dear, such as your significant other, or any relative, colleague, or associate. Ensure transparency and candor when communicating your decision. This psychological enhancement holds significant importance. Nevertheless, in the event of a falling out or the absence of said individuals, there exists the peril of seamlessly reverting back to previous habits. Hence, it is imperative to have multiple contingency plans readily available.

Talk to others. An additional strategy involves fostering an environment that dissuades individuals, including others, from engaging in smoking activities. This fosters a perception of self-awareness that becomes operational whenever you feel the urge to smoke, thereby empowering you to refrain from smoking as a sign of consideration towards others.

Discover a valid justification to cease. Undertake this task for personal betterment, for the welfare of your kin, for the benefit of your acquaintances, for the sake of affection, and in consideration of the preservation of the environment. Discover a purpose, a justification, any motivation to cease. Include it in your list of desired experiences.

Get cured... Peruse this literary work and similar compositions... Acquire knowledge and receive expert guidance to combat and prevent cigarette addiction. We could engage in an extended intellectual and ethical debate regarding the initial assertion, however, ultimately I am confident that I can successfully persuade you that smoking does not directly cause fatalities, rather it is the individual who partakes in smoking that ultimately brings about their own demise. While an opportunity remains available and your potential for redemption persists, it is advised that you take immediate action to safeguard yourself.

Simple Mental Exercises.

A study was conducted on a global scale, involving 2000 participants of both genders from various countries. The study encompassed a series of cognitive tasks, and the findings indicated an average success rate of 80%. Variables such as the mean age of the individuals, their smoking habits, patterns of living, financial status, racial background, demographic factors, as well as their social and health conditions were accounted for.

There are situations in which the act of smoking cigarettes is regarded as a factor that instigates heightened alcohol consumption. There is contention among individuals regarding the correlation between smoking and alcohol consumption, with the claim being that the quantity of cigarettes consumed tends to escalate when individuals partake in drinking alcohol. In light of this situation, what measures can be undertaken to discontinue smoking while continuing the consumption of alcoholic beverages? To address this inquiry, let us examine the assertions posited by Dr. Sanders in her publication, Heart and Lungs.

The excessive consumption of alcohol is tantamount in its addictive capacity to behaviors such as smoking or substance abuse. Nonetheless, it should be noted that the disparity lies in the disparity between alcoholism and cigarette smoking. Specifically, the development of chronic addiction tends to be a prolonged process in the case of smoking, whereas alcoholism can manifest at a faster pace, primarily prompted by factors like stress, lack of access to counseling and support services, peer pressure, and environmental influences.

An individual may persistently exhibit alcoholic tendencies over a significant period of time without engaging in excessive smoking. Likewise, a person can maintain a smoking habit for years without becoming a habitual drunkard.

Typically, individuals tend to indulge in a significant quantity of cigarettes in conjunction with alcoholic beverages when experiencing elevated levels of stress or in a communal setting. In such circumstances. There is a prevalent association between complementary smoking, which occurs when one smokes while consuming alcoholic beverages, and recreational, social, or stress-triggered circumstances.

What is the underlying reason behind the tendency of individuals who consume alcohol to engage in frequent smoking? Could it be described as a state of exhilaration, unease, or despondency? Upon examining numerous instances, Dr. Sanders unequivocally asserts that the act of partaking in alcohol in social settings (i.e., consuming alcoholic beverages in the presence of one or more individuals) is more commonly correlated with an elevated likelihood of smoking multiple cigarettes, as compared to consuming alcohol alone. However, smoking in the company of colleagues, regardless of your alcohol consumption, appears to elevate the quantity of cigarettes you consume. You are more prone to willingly accept a cigarette that is proffered by an individual with whom you share some connection, such as a friend, a coworker, or an acquaintance, thereby increasing your exposure and vulnerability to smoking, compared to the likelihood of doing so when you are alone or in the presence of non-smokers. Another factor that proponents linking drinking to increased smoking often overlook is the correlation between simultaneous smoking and drinking, which can be attributed to an individual's level of excitement or lack thereof. Consequently, this behavior can be seen as an unconscious or conscious effort to enhance their mood. It is noteworthy that, according to a study involving 700 participants who placed bets on football pools in the UK, smokers demonstrated a tendency to consume fewer alcoholic beverages and smoke fewer cigarettes when they won a bet and were present in a bar with friends or peers. Conversely, when individuals incurred losses and found themselves in comparable settings, they showed a proclivity to consume more alcohol and smoke a greater number of cigarettes. Likewise, it is observed that professional gamblers who are smokers tend to imbibe alcohol to a lesser extent and indulge in smoking less frequently while experiencing victories. However, during unfortunate evenings characterized by losses, the opposite pattern emerges. In general, individuals employ smoking as a means of substituting for emotional lacking, fulfilling inner desires for contentment, and symbolizing the culmination of an action, event, or segment of their day.

Try having Smoking days...

Individuals do not universally consume an identical quantity of cigarettes on a daily basis. There are occasions when an individual smokes in greater or lesser quantities. For individuals seeking to cease smoking, it is advisable to commence monitoring the daily quantity of cigarettes consumed. This will cultivate within you a heightened awareness of self whenever you engage in smoking. One may find themselves involuntarily contemplating whether or not to partake in the act of smoking this particular item. What is the current count of cigarettes I have consumed today? What if I defer it to a later time, or postpone it until tomorrow? Please ascertain the days on which you have consumed a higher quantity of cigarettes as well as the days on which you indulge in smoking later than usual. Establish a cognitive log or diligently transcribe the timetables, occurrences, and engagements that contributed to the disparity in the quantity of cigarettes consumed across various days. Furthermore, endeavor to gravitate towards activities that diminish the likelihood of engaging in smoking. Motivate yourself to acknowledge any progress made in cultivating your abstinent lifestyle.

Learn to delay....

Please consider retaining the cigarette in your grasp for a few moments prior to igniting it. By clutching it, your mind receives a similar subliminal signal, as if you were in possession of your cigarette. What is the reason for the urgency?

When procrastination pays off...

Don't buy in cartons. Please ensure you possess the fewest number of cigarette sticks with you as feasible. I used to have an acquaintance who would purchase a pack of cigarettes, meticulously choose a mere one or two to retain within the package, and subsequently discard the remaining tobacco sticks.

The pack nestled in his pocket provided him with a sense of readiness, an assurance that he would be equipped for a smoke if the desire presented itself; however, he would need to exercise discretion in selecting the opportune moment. Does the current moment indicate that it is appropriate to engage in the act of smoking? Should I consider it a waste if I were to consume this cigarette at this moment?

And he will persistently contemplate his course of action within his thoughts, often leading him to eventually persuade himself to refrain from igniting and partaking in smoking until a subsequent moment, thereby gradually diminishing his impulsive inclination to smoke and suppressing his temporary urge.

Refrain from storing cigarettes in your vehicle... Is that yet another spurious argument? However, it exhibits a high level of efficacy. Refrain from granting yourself convenient and immediate availability to cigarettes. Please refrain from keeping cigarettes in your vehicle. Remove the discarded cigarette remnants from your vehicle and eliminate the lingering scent of tobacco in your car. Guess what? The sensory nerves located in your nasal passages will undergo a process of adaptation to the surrounding environment, resulting in a decreased ability to detect the odors commonly described by cigarette smokers as musty, stale, twangy, or stuffy within enclosed areas. Liberate yourself from enclosed areas that retain the scent of tobacco. The visual and olfactory stimuli emanating from a preferred brand of cigarettes can serve as triggering factors for individuals who smoke. They suddenly recall that they have abstained from smoking throughout the day, or they appear to experience an abrupt urge to engage in smoking.

When individuals who engage in smoking are not subject to premature mortality...

Exclusively by ceasing prematurely! By exercising restraint and mindfulness towards the irresistible temptations that compel you to succumb to a habit that revolves around smoking. When one becomes consciously aware of their obligation and accountability in maintaining their own well-being and fostering the possibility of an extended lifespan. Certain individuals assert that they have acquired the habit of smoking due to the influence of their parents, mentors, or esteemed figures, yet such justifications are unsubtle and implausible. I concur that individuals do not possess the authority to impose their personal decisions on others, particularly in circumstances concerning matters of life and death. Smoking is inherently an issue of mortal consequences, with imminent mortality and inevitable health complications prevailing. However, you have the ability to alter the equilibrium. You hold the aces. With a slight exertion, you can tip the balance in your favor. Smoking unjustly deprives individuals of their lives.

Is Nicotine Replacement Therapy A Suitable Option For You?

Individuals with a high degree of nicotine dependence are advised to consider undergoing nicotine replacement therapy. These individuals have a propensity to consume at minimum one full packet of cigarettes on a daily basis. They may even arise during nocturnal hours solely for the purpose of engaging in the act of smoking. In addition, they frequently initiate smoking immediately upon awakening in the morning. Regardless of their physical state or overall well-being, they will proceed to smoke a cigarette.

Conversely, individuals who smoke fewer than ten cigarettes per day may not experience the desired efficacy from nicotine replacement therapy. This approach is particularly tailored for individuals who heavily depend on cigarettes or tobacco merchandise. Additionally, this product is not intended for individuals who continue to engage in smoking. It will be effective only after they cease.

Per the information provided by the United States Agency for Healthcare Research and Quality, it is not recommended for pregnant women, adolescents, and individuals using specific medications to utilize nicotine replacement therapy. Ensure that you possess adequate knowledge concerning the potential hazards associated with this treatment.

What type of smoker do you identify as?

In accordance with the severity of one's smoking habit, it is typically advised to consider utilizing nicotine replacement therapy products. If an individual consumes less than ten cigarettes on a daily basis, they can be considered a light smoker. If an individual consumes a minimum of one pack of cigarettes on a daily basis, they can be classified as a habitual smoker. If you are situated within the middle range, you can be classified as an average smoker.

If you happen to engage in smokeless tobacco use, you might discover that specific forms of nicotine replacement therapy are relatively more efficacious compared to others. For example, one could utilize nicotine lozenges and gums. These products will enable you to regulate your dosage effectively, thereby mitigating your cravings.

Typically, nicotine replacement therapy products are designated for individuals who engage in smoking. Hence, individuals who engage in the use of smokeless tobacco products may encounter challenges in appropriately determining their dosage. However, it is imperative that you strive for a dosage that approximates the nicotine content derived from tobacco in order to mitigate the onset of withdrawal symptoms.

Individuals who engage in pronounced tobacco consumption typically exceed a quantity of three pouches of tobacco or three cans of snuff on a weekly basis. Typically, they employ a more elevated dosage of nicotine replacement therapy. Snuff and chew are illustrative of smokeless tobacco products.

However, individuals who consume a smaller quantity of two to three pouches or cans per week may consider using a moderate dosage. Individuals whose consumption of pouches or cans falls below two per week are eligible to administer the minimum prescribed dosage.

"Strategies for Selecting an Appropriate Nicotine Replacement Therapy

No single form of nicotine replacement therapy demonstrates superiority over the others. When it comes to product selection, one should take into account their individual requirements, preferences, and way of life. It is also essential to take into account your smoking behavior, including the type of tobacco product you consume, be it cigarettes or smokeless tobacco. Furthermore, it is important to consider your preference regarding tactile interaction with the product as well as oral consumption. It is essential to take convenience and user-friendliness into consideration.

Nicotine lozenges, inhalers, and gums are oral administration options for delivering the product into the oral cavity. They enable individuals to regulate their dosages and effectively manage their cravings. Usually, lozenges and gums are devoid of sugar. Therefore, individuals with diabetes can confidently utilize them without risk. To obtain complete assurance, it would be advisable to consult both your physician and the manufacturer.

Nicotine nasal sprays are highly advantageous for individuals seeking immediate outcomes. Inhalers allow individuals to replicate the act of smoking tobacco or cigarettes by manually grasping and inhaling from them. Patches are convenient. They solely necessitate one usage per day. On the other hand, individuals with specific medical conditions or allergies may be contraindicated from utilizing nasal sprays, patches, or inhalers. It is advisable to refrain from utilizing nicotine gums in cases where one has dental work or dentures, as they possess an inclination to adhere to such surfaces, leading to complications during the chewing process.

Regardless of the specific nicotine replacement therapy you opt for, ensure that you adhere strictly to the recommended duration of usage. Seek guidance from your physician in case you possess any uncertainties, inquiries, or apprehensions, as well as if you intend to merge one product with another.

Furthermore, it is imperative that you obtain the consent of your physician should you desire to engage in high-dose nicotine replacement therapy. Typically, substantial quantities of nicotine are generally necessary for this approach. It is employed to administer a higher quantity of nicotine to smokers, surpassing their typical intake from conventional cigarettes. Access to it may be prohibited for individuals with cardiovascular diseases or other medical conditions.

Challenges

Similar to any established routine in your daily existence, particularly one upon which your physical well-being has grown reliant, adversities will inevitably arise. When one chooses to cease smoking, one must confront the physiological as well as the psychological ramifications. From a psychological standpoint, the challenge is formidable as the habit has seamlessly integrated into your everyday existence, and has become deeply entrenched within your established regimen. Implementing this alteration would result in a sense of unmistakable deprivation.

Nicotine withdrawal

Your decision to quit smoking will greatly benefit your physical well-being;

however, it may take some time before you begin to experience these positive effects. Initially, your body will undergo a state of shock, resulting in a probable manifestation of several commonly encountered symptoms associated with nicotine withdrawal.

Some of these include:

Depression

Headaches

Irritability

Nausea

Stomach problems

Tiredness

Insomnia

Lack of concentration

Increased hunger

Anger

Proceed gradually in your journey, as the passage of each day without smoking will result in a gradual reduction of these withdrawal symptoms. Discover methods of mitigating the manifestations via recreational activities, physical exertion, and interpersonal engagements. Engage in conversations with individuals who have experienced similar circumstances and attentively heed their counsel. Simultaneously, it is crucial to bear in mind that each process of recuperation is distinct, and every individual will undergo their own unique expedition.

Numerous individuals who indulge in smoking will attest to a phenomenon whereby they encounter a perceived alteration in the flow of time, wherein it appears to decelerate significantly. Just like any unpleasant aspect of life, the passage of time will inevitably appear interminable. Do not remain idle during this period. Ensure that you engage in activities that fill your time to the maximum extent possible, and approach each day with a steadfast and measured approach.

Preventing weight gain

Cigarette smoke contains nicotine, which effectively elevates the body's metabolic rate and leads to a heightened calorie burn compared to the regular baseline. Regrettably, numerous individuals perceive this as an incentive to initiate smoking and as a justification for abstaining from quitting. Nevertheless, this approach to weight loss is highly unnatural as it involves elevating your heart rate by 10 to 20 beats per minute, which can potentially culminate in the development of heart failure or cardiovascular ailments.

There are two prevailing factors as to why individuals who cease smoking often experience weight gain. First, their food consumption remains unchanged, yet their metabolic rate has decelerated. Secondly, they exhibit increased food consumption as a means of substituting the act of smoking. This occurrence is quite customary, however, it can be readily averted. Above all, it is imperative that this does not serve as a justification to persist in smoking. There exist considerably more viable and enduring methods to maintain a slender physique. Frequently, the underlying factor is not solely related to the cuisine itself; rather, it pertains to the fundamental need for a means to engage or content oneself. Outlined below are several strategies that can be employed to circumvent weight gain:

Chewing gum can offer solace by engaging in the simple act of oral stimulation. A form of distraction.

Undertake meal planning - set aside time each week to meticulously plan your meals in advance. It is not imperative to be excessively meticulous, but possessing knowledge about your food inventory and ensuring adequate quantities is of utmost importance. Doing so will prevent impulsive choices and enable prudent decision-making. Take advantage of this opportunity to incorporate wholesome and natural nourishment into your lifestyle. Please bear in mind that you are embarking on a path towards improving your health and well-being, thus it is advisable not to replace smoking with unhealthy eating habits. You will effectively initiate a new dependency that will require your diligent efforts to overcome.

Opt for nutritious snacks - ensure that you consistently have an assortment of snacks available to satiate your appetite. Always ensure to consume smaller, frequent meals throughout the day rather than waiting until extreme hunger strikes. Some viable alternatives for nutritious snacks are yogurt, fresh fruit, popcorn that is air-popped, assorted nuts, and vegetables accompanied by hummus, among others. Commence physical activity by mobilizing your body - it is now opportune to engage in exercise once more. You will notice a decline in the health of your lungs compared to their previous state. Therefore, it is advisable to begin with a conservative approach and gradually enhance your exercise routine on a weekly basis. Discover methods of mobility that are well-suited to your individual needs and preferences. Enroll in a fitness center, engage in regular jogging, enroll in a physical fitness course, or commence a cycling routine. If none of these options are suitable, it is important to bear in mind that physical activity extends beyond traditional workouts. Instead, explore alternative methods to enhance your level of physical movement. Engage in leisurely strolling within a shopping mall vicinity or a nearby neighborhood, or partake in gardening activities and undertake household cleaning tasks. Additionally, it is important to bear in mind that implementing minor modifications in your daily routine, such as opting for the stairs rather than the escalator, can be worthwhile.

Ensure that you diligently engage in the practice of dental hygiene, as it is expected that you are already familiar with this routine. Nevertheless, an effective strategy for preventing overeating entails the act of brushing your teeth upon experiencing a craving. You will likely observe a reduction in both the desire to smoke and the desire to consume food.

Engage in planned recreational pursuits - frequently, we tend to consume food out of a sense of tedium, thereby misinterpreting that ennui as actual hunger. Hence, ensure that you engage in various tasks and meticulously organize your schedule.

Consume water - the consumption of water will help you maintain hydration and a feeling of satiety for an extended period of time.

Maintain a positive mindset – keep in mind the reasons behind your actions and the immense gratitude your body will undoubtedly express towards you. Offer yourself a well-deserved incentive upon successfully achieving each milestone.

Relapse

You've done everything. You have selected an approach that aligns with your preferences, navigated through the obstacles, and demonstrated commendable performance. Then suddenly, you relapse. The majority of relapses transpire within the initial week or two after cessation; however, it is important to acknowledge that such occurrences are not limited to any specific timeframe. The majority of individuals experience a relapse due to the misconception that indulging in a single instance would not have detrimental effects. Nevertheless, an individual is not solely defined as a singular entity, and consequently, one may inevitably become entangled once again within the confines of the identical destructive cycle.

I have experienced a relapse. What steps should I take from here?

In the initial stages, it is crucial to avoid being unduly critical of oneself. This is a highly prevalent occurrence that does not serve as an indicator of your identity or undermine your resilience and moral fiber.

Do not allow a single setback to derail your entire objective. Pause and reflect on the initial reasons that led to your decision to discontinue.

Talk to someone. Do not feel embarrassed by the occurrence of a relapse.

Please document the specific occurrence and underlying cause of the relapse. Please provide comprehensive and elaborate descriptions, explicitly outlining the sequence of emotions experienced, ranging from the initial craving for the cigarette, through the duration of smoking it, until the conclusion of the smoking experience.

Take a deep breath. Start again.

Implement proactive measures to prevent its recurrence. If you believed that you possessed the fortitude to retain cigarettes within the premises, then it would be advisable to dispose of them. Create challenges for yourself in order to discourage smoking.

Being in a relationship with an individual who engages in smoking habits

Merely committing to quit smoking does not guarantee that your partner, friends, and family will follow suit. While certain individuals can manage to limit their exposure to other individuals who smoke to a certain extent, it can be more challenging for others, particularly those who reside in close proximity to a smoker. It is not within your purview to effect change upon them, and regrettably, if they are unwilling to relinquish their stance, your options for intervention are limited.

While it is not within your authority to request that they cease their actions, you may engage in a conversation with them where you sincerely communicate your intention to resign and provide them with an explanation for your decision. It is of utmost importance to request their utmost mindfulness in regards to this matter. One advantage of this situation is that acquiring the ability to quit smoking while cohabiting with a smoker will render most other social circumstances more manageable than anticipated.

The paramount factor in this context pertains to the cultivation of transparent and sincere dialogue between individuals who smoke and those who do not. Please ensure that you clarify that your intention is not to force them to quit, but rather to inquire if they would be willing to make certain concessions, such as avoiding leaving cigarettes unattended or refraining from smoking in your presence. During the initial stages, particularly when you are susceptible to even the slightest aroma of tobacco.

Please be reminded that this is a personal endeavor, and it would be advisable to refrain from unnecessarily involving others in order to avoid complicating the situation. However, it is conceivable that your positive habits may eventually influence them as well.

Avail Yourself Of All Available Assistance

Allow others to assist you

As mentioned previously, quitting smoking can be significantly challenging if undertaken without any external assistance or support. Ensure that you avail yourself of all available assistance from individuals in your proximity. There are numerous methods available to accomplish this.

For instance, you may inform your family members, friends, and colleagues of your conscious decision to cease smoking, while seeking their valuable support. According to research findings, it has been demonstrated that your chances of achieving success in your smoking cessation objectives are significantly enhanced when you possess...

some help..

You may contemplate enrolling in telephone, group, or individual counseling services. Engaging in counseling can significantly enhance the probability of achieving success. This can additionally assist you in recognizing and conquering circumstances that may elicit the inclination to ignite a tobacco product. Currently, free programs can be accessed at local health centers and hospitals. You may contact the local health department for information regarding the programs available in your vicinity. If you happen to reside in the United States, there is also toll-free telecommunication available.

counseling being offered.

You may also consider seeking assistance from your healthcare provider, such as a physician, dentist, pharmacist, nurse, psychologist, or a professional specializing in smoking cessation counseling or coaching, particularly if you are interested in exploring the potential benefits of medication.

You may also integrate the utilization of prescribed or over-the-counter medications in conjunction with cessation counseling. This combination demonstrates enhanced efficacy relative to either individual method when used independently.

It is crucial to secure the assistance of individuals in your vicinity, as without their support, achieving victory in this conflict will undoubtedly be unattainable. With their assistance, things will become easier for you and the difficulty of the challenge will diminish compared to its initial appearance.

CHAPTER SEVEN

Planning for Relapse

Relapse prevention is arguably the paramount element in the smoking cessation puzzle for individuals seeking to abandon this habit. An array of approaches are utilized in the preparations for relapse. This encompasses ensuring that the premises remain completely free of smoking at all times. Individuals who engage in this practice on a regular basis commonly attest to its efficacy in averting a relapse in their addictive behavior. Here are some additional techniques that can help you maintain a tobacco-free lifestyle:

Individuals who are prone to relapse should make concerted efforts to minimize their smoking activity until the desire to smoke becomes sufficiently intense for them to yield to it. You may discover that abstaining from holding a cigarette while making an effort to quit smoking can potentially facilitate the process. Furthermore, it is imperative to acknowledge that cessation without the support of a healthcare professional is consistently linked to an elevated likelihood of experiencing a resumption of the addictive behavior.

Formulate a Strategy for Relapse Prevention: Establishing a well-structured plan for smoking cessation is an integral aspect of preventing relapses. This is commonly termed as a disengagement strategy in certain professional contexts. One aspect of this plan could involve implementing a communication mechanism wherein individuals can indicate to their family or acquaintances that they have received an urgent call. There exists a potential scenario wherein, upon discovering your smoking habit, they may be inclined to request that you cease. One might consider taking a respite from their customary activities by venturing to a location devoid of enticing distractions.

Identify the factors that cause stress for you and endeavor to develop effective strategies to manage them instead of succumbing to the inclination to smoke when stressed. There are multiple approaches to achieve this objective, with meditation emerging as the most efficacious method. Engaging in meditation can foster mindfulness and enhance capacity to manage stress. Meditation may be engaged in at any given time and in any place, rendering it a superb choice for individuals seeking additional support in maintaining abstinence. If you have not yet undertaken this endeavor, this location serves as a favorable initial point of initiation.

Exploring and implementing advantageous methods for managing stress is advisable. It may be justifiable to entertain the inclination to smoke as a sole mechanism for emotional regulation. Therapeutic interventions can aid in the cultivation of effective coping strategies. The mindfulness technique, elucidated more extensively in the referenced materials, has demonstrated efficacy in various circumstances.

Establishing a support system of individuals to rely upon. Support systems can provide assistance in managing stress, handling triggers, offering encouragement in moments of decision to abstain, and accomplishing a range of other tasks and engagements. The notion that one must not disregard is that individuals who require cessation vary in their circumstances and characteristics. Certain individuals may experience greater ease when receiving support from a sizable group of individuals, whereas others may discover that a smaller support network, such as an online community consisting of individuals who share their goal of quitting, proves more advantageous to them.

The chosen date for smoking cessation:

Ensure thorough readiness for a day of refraining and the preceding days by diligently undertaking all necessary measures to achieve optimal preparedness. "You are advised to undertake the following actions:

Prior to your designated cessation date, allocate a span of several days for self-reflection and nurturing connections within your support system. It can be advantageous to anticipate your designated day of cessation by formulating a list of tasks to be accomplished. Some items to consider including on the list are:

Develop a comprehensive strategy for oneself in the event of encountering stimuli that may provoke a response, including managing stress and addressing challenging circumstances. The more adequately equipped you are, the greater the likelihood of successfully managing your impulses when they arise.

Arrange for someone to be present to provide support on the day you choose to quit. What will be the composition of your support network? Will you be availing yourself of assistance from your network of support? What are your intended activities for the day?

What is your agenda for the day? For instance, in the event that you intend to partake in a support group wherein individuals who grasp your experiences gather, it is advisable to take this into account. Shall you undergo admission at the hospital or at the drug rehabilitation center? Are you planning to seek out a nearby support group for yourself?

Ascertain which techniques will yield the greatest advantages for you as you commence your cessation process. The utilization of the patch, nicotine gum, and NRT collectively enhance the likelihood of achieving desired outcomes. However, does it yield a discernible impact? In an alternative scenario, what if you were to utilize the patch in tandem with nicotine gum?

What would be the most suitable choice for you?

Establish a network of assistance that will be available to you on the day you cease your activities and in the future. What strategies or approaches do you believe will afford you the greatest likelihood of achieving success? Would you be interested in soliciting the assistance of a select group of individuals who are already cognizant of your intentions? Would you be open to the prospect of engaging in a collaborative partnership with a potential sponsor? Would you be open to seeking guidance and gaining a deeper understanding of your cessation strategy? Would you be interested in reconnecting with a support group with which you were previously affiliated? Would you be willing to consider alternative perspectives? Would you prefer to engage in a conversation with an abstinence coach or contact a hotline specifically dedicated to smoking cessation?

Grant yourself the virtue of exhibiting patience towards yourself. You possess great perseverance and resilience. It will be necessary for you to surrender. There is an extensive list of tasks that need to be accomplished within the span of one day. It is impractical to anticipate relinquishing your employment.

Establish a reliable network of assistance that will be available to you on the occasion that you opt to abstain from smoking. Should you choose to cease smoking, you cannot consistently depend on the support of your loved ones, acquaintances, or medical professionals. It is imperative that you establish a self-sufficient framework to aid you in your cessation efforts. Access to a support system in which you are surrounded by others who are also attempting to quit smoking is essential for success.

In Order To Terminate One's Engagement, It Is Imperative To Contemplate This Matter Critically.

SELF-ESTEEM

According to the pronouncement of the World Health Organization (WHO), a conclusive correlation exists between self-esteem, self-perception, and tobacco consumption. It is, therefore, not difficult to comprehend why smokers possess a diminished sense of self-worth at their core.

Individuals who engage in smoking tend to exhibit a passive disposition when it comes to harboring anticipations for the future. They engage in smoking as a means to promptly alleviate their present stress, displaying indifference towards potential long-term ramifications.

Nevertheless, it is noted that younger smokers exhibit higher levels of self-esteem compared to their older counterparts. The perspective of teenagers towards their peers, including classmates, friends, girlfriends, and boyfriends who engage in smoking, is frequently perceived as sophisticated, mature, and developed by their counterparts who deeply yearn to exchange roles with their smoking acquaintances.

THEY LIED TO YOU!

Whilst targeting young individuals with smoking products, marketers frequently convey the message that smoking is regarded as a fashionable activity. In spite of these marketing tactics, individuals have developed a heightened awareness of the adverse effects of smoking on their social welfare. Indeed, there is a growing inclination among contemporary adolescents to cease the habit of smoking, primarily due to its detrimental effects on their social interactions. Indeed, what kind of impression does your smoking habit create about you?

Due to the exorbitant cost associated with certain smoking paraphernalia, smokers incur substantial expenses to acquire them. Consequently, they engage in deficit spending in other significant endeavors.

In areas designated for non-smoking, a smoker may find themselves compelled to interrupt their activities due to an inability to maintain focus. Instances in which individuals are deprived of opportunities for respite, such as during periods of prolonged air travel, can prove discomfiting as they experience a compelling desire for a cigarette that cannot be satisfied.

Upon conducting interviews with several individuals who do not engage in smoking, it was discovered that they expressed a lack of admiration for the presence of individuals who engage in smoking in close proximity to them. Smokers frequently encounter disapproving gazes from individuals who are unwilling to be subjected to their secondhand smoke.

Certain individuals may choose to abstain from purchasing automobiles or properties from individuals who engage in smoking within their vehicles or residences, as prospective buyers may have a strong aversion to driving in a car or residing in a dwelling that retains the scent of tobacco.

There are individuals who also believe that individuals who smoke exhibit lower intelligence and demonstrate a lack of concern for their future well-being.

Being employed in a workplace where the manager emits an aroma of smoke and tobacco can frequently prove bothersome to individuals on the staff who do not partake in smoking. Notwithstanding the considerable potential possessed by a staff member, they may still encounter challenges when it comes to performing their duties with optimal efficiency.

The aforementioned items are currently en route to your location.

The chemical compounds found in cigarettes, namely nicotine and cyanide, are significantly implicated in the adverse effects imposed on our physical health. However, our bodies engage in diligent efforts to expel these harmful chemicals promptly once they are detected. Regrettably, our physiological systems lack the sophistication necessary to consistently eliminate all injurious substances upon ingestion.

Once our bodies reach a point where they are unable to eliminate these chemicals, they promptly begin to experience the effects of poisoning. And the outcome is readily apparent: over an extended duration, our physique manifests health issues such as cardiovascular diseases, emphysema, cerebrovascular accidents, and various forms of cancer including those affecting the throat, bladder, and stomach. Additionally, individuals who smoke face an elevated susceptibility to respiratory infections such as pneumonia and bronchitis. These illnesses have the potential to curtail an individual's ability to function and perform regular tasks, which can result in fatality in numerous instances. In the United States, smoking is responsible for one-fifth of all fatalities.

Smoking significantly contributes to a reduction in bone density, thereby heightening the susceptibility to osteoporosis, a condition that makes the bones of elderly individuals more prone to fracturing and increasing the likelihood of developing a stooped posture. Moreover, when comparing smokers to nonsmokers, it can be observed that smokers exhibit diminished levels of physical activity due to a notable reduction in lung capacity.

Notably, smoking has the potential to impact fertility issues and can have adverse effects on sexual well-being for both males and females. In the event that females utilizing certain forms of contraception engage in smoking, they may potentially experience severe health complications such as cardiac events.

Consequently, these enumerated are several enduring health repercussions associated with smoking. In addition to the aforementioned long-term consequences, smoking can also give rise to issues such as:

Bad skin

Bad breadth

Unpleasant odor emanating from garments and hair.

Reduced athletic performance

Increased susceptibility to harm and prolonged duration of recovery.

Increased likelihood of illness

The inhalation of "passive smoke" poses significant harm to individuals who do not smoke, as their susceptibility to developing cancer or cardiovascular diseases increases by approximately 25%.

Chapter 3: The Advantages of Adopting a Smoke-Free Lifestyle

Abstaining from smoking enables individuals to enhance their prospects for longer, healthier, and more enriched lives. The specific age at which an individual initiated smoking, as well as their current age, holds negligible significance. The utmost significance lies in the fact that opting to cease implies opting for an enhanced existence.

Ceasing the act of smoking effectively mitigates an individual's susceptibility to the development of various ailments and conditions, notably influenza, pneumonia, myocardial infarctions, malignancies, and cerebrovascular accidents. Upon cessation of smoking, immediate improvements in health can be observed among individuals across all age groups, irrespective of whether they are currently afflicted by smoking-induced ailments.

Ceasing the activity for approximately 20 minutes can restore your heart rate and abnormally elevated blood pressure to a state of normalcy. Following approximately 12 hours of smoking cessation, the concentration of carbon monoxide in your system, a compound that hinders the blood's capacity to transport oxygen, will commence a gradual decline.

Within a short span of a few weeks, significant improvements can be observed in the enhancement of your circulation. You can expect a resolution to your excessive phlegm production, as your pulmonary function has been enhanced. Over the course of several months, the act of quitting smoking can further enhance your lung capacity, thereby alleviating respiratory distress and mitigating the likelihood of contracting infections.

Quitting smoking for a year would reduce your likelihood of developing coronary heart disease or experiencing a heart attack by 50%. Over a span of five years, a considerable decrease in the likelihood of developing cancers affecting the throat, mouth, stomach, bladder, cervix, and esophagus is observed. You exhibit a medical state that closely resembles that of an individual who has never engaged in smoking. After a decade, the likelihood of succumbing to lung cancer is reduced by 50%, alongside a notable decrease in the susceptibility to pancreatic and laryngeal malignancies. After a period of 15 years since your cessation of smoking, your susceptibility to experiencing coronary heart disease is equivalent to that of an individual who has never engaged in smoking.

These represent just a few of the numerous advantages that can be obtained upon making a resolute commitment to permanently cease the act of smoking. Instant gratification will also be bestowed upon you upon your decision to discard those parcels containing tobacco and cigarettes. Your oral hygiene would be improved, resulting in fresher breath and a brighter smile.

Within a fortnight, the choice you make will lead to a reversal of the visible effects of skin aging, presenting a younger and rejuvenated appearance. The sensory receptors in your nasal and oral cavities will initiate a process of regeneration, thereby augmenting your gustatory perception and restoring your olfactory function to its regular state. Additionally, there is no longer a need for concern regarding engaging in daily tasks which you believe may result in breathlessness.

By abstaining from smoking, one effectively extends their lifespan, thereby avoiding the health complications associated with continued tobacco use.

Chapter 4: Strategies for Cessation of Smoking Habits

Engaging in a lifestyle free from smoking does not guarantee a life devoid of stress. Indeed, stress frequently serves as a catalyst for individuals resorting to smoking; however, it is imperative to acknowledge that nicotine is an ill-advised solution for dealing with one's myriad challenges. There exist numerous approaches to managing stress, and smoking should not be considered as a viable option in this regard.

If you are contemplating the state of your well-being and desiring an improved way of living, then proceed to embark upon the initial stage. Choose to quit smoking. The only course of action available is to proceed by reaching a decision. There exist a multitude of approaches that can be employed to cease the habit of smoking. Certain options may indeed exhibit superior qualities compared to others; however, the paramount consideration lies in selecting the optimal approach that you can genuinely attain. What is required is a combination of determination and unwavering commitment.

Many individuals desire to resign, but are uncertain about the procedure. It is essential to understand that there exists no definitive approach to resigning, yet there are measures one can undertake to effectively achieve a successful departure.

Examine all the factors contributing to your preference for smoking.

Please obtain a pen and paper, and proceed to enumerate both your preferences and dislikes pertaining to the act of smoking. If you believe yourself to possess the required courage, you may inquire of your acquaintances and loved ones about their displeasures related to your smoking tendencies. If the adverse aspect holds greater significance in your perspective, then you are prepared to resign.

Pick a Quit Date

Establish a specific date and formulate a comprehensive strategy for your forthcoming course of action. You may also include both your own signature and the signature of your witness with regard to your intended plans. Selecting a specific date to cease one's actions holds considerable significance; however, it is advisable to refrain from designating a date that is excessively distant. Over time, you may come to alter your perspective. Ensure that you allocate sufficient time for the completion of necessary preparations. You may opt to select either a randomly chosen date or one that holds personal significance for you. You must remain dedicated.

Prepare to Quit

Acquiring packs of cigarettes will not be conducive to your efforts to cease smoking. In lieu of transporting a backpack, you choose to bear several sticks during your ventures. Upon experiencing the urge to smoke once more, you will swiftly realize the dearth of cigarettes at your disposal. This will effectively assist you in reducing your cigarette consumption and smoking fewer cigarettes on a daily basis.

Keep Yourself Busy

Compile a comprehensive inventory outlining the range of actions one can undertake in response to the onset of cravings. One may engage in activities such as embarking on a leisurely stroll, enjoying meaningful moments with one's significant other, hydrating with a refreshing glass of water, engaging in playtime with a canine companion, tending to household chores, immersing oneself in literary pursuits, indulging in a soothing warm bath, catching up on rest with a gentle slumber, or simply finding solace in a deep inhalation. Distracting yourself helps. While present in the workplace, individuals have the option to utilize their computer for leisure or endeavor to contact an acquaintance.

Get Rid of Temptation

As the date of your cessation draws near, dispose of all items that could serve as reminders of smoking. Please ensure the removal of any remaining cigarettes, ashtrays, lighters, and matches from the table, your room, and even your vehicle. Make a concerted effort to distance yourself from sources of temptation, including both individuals and environments that have the potential to lure you astray. You will quickly discover an enhanced ability to manage these circumstances with greater ease.

Indulge in the Pleasure of Savoring a Delicate Herbal Infusion

Partaking in a cup of tea serves as a viable substitute for indulging in a cigarette. It is available for consumption during breakfast, lunch, or following the evening meal. Commence the steeping of tea leaves and indulge in a sip. A single cup has the potential to alleviate stress in a similar manner to the effects of nicotine.

Grab Some Snacks

Rather than allowing your hands to grasp a cigarette, endeavor to submerge it into a bowl of nutritious nuts or alternative wholesome snacks. You may opt to consume sunflower seeds, pistachio nuts, or even celery sticks as a viable alternative, particularly when you are conscious of your weight. Alternatively, you may opt for the use of substitutes such as lollipops or toothpicks infused with cinnamon to adhere to your mouth. Confectioneries and chewing gums devoid of sugar can similarly alleviate your yearnings.

Implement Modifications to Your Daily Schedule

To mitigate one's cravings, engage in a slight modification of one's habits. Please consider relocating to an alternative seating arrangement, exiting the premises and engaging in a leisurely stroll, or embarking on an exploration of unfamiliar pathways during your daily commute. If you engage in the practice of smoking in the morning alongside a cup of coffee, consider substituting your beverage of choice with tea. Additionally, you have the option to visit a coffee establishment that enforces a no-smoking policy, as well as offers a selection of food options that are less likely to induce cravings for smoking.

Establish a Smoke-free Area

In order to prevent succumbing to the habit of smoking, it is important to refrain from allowing individuals to ignite cigarettes or use tobacco within the confines of your residence or vehicle. One may consider displaying a signage indicating "Smoking is Prohibited". Additionally, it is recommended to politely communicate with your acquaintances to refrain from smoking in close proximity while dining at a restaurant. Designate your premises as a completely smoke-free area.

Visit a Therapist

Seek out a therapist who can facilitate your exploration of the optimal approach to cessation. Behavioral therapy possesses the potential to assist in the cessation of smoking through its capability to identify the stimuli that prompt smoking behavior, while also facilitating the development of strategies to diminish cravings. Provision of emotional support would also be extended whenever it becomes necessary.

Nicotine replacement therapy is most effective when combined with behavioral therapy, although it should be noted that minors must seek explicit permission from their healthcare provider before embarking on this therapeutic approach. This operational method primarily entails the utilization of nicotine gums, inhalers, patches, and sprays. It provides a nicotine dosage devoid of tobacco consumption, thus increasing the probability of cessation among individuals subjected to this therapeutic approach.

Find Support

Certain individuals have managed to successfully cease their smoking habits without reliance on specific pharmaceutical interventions or external support. There are numerous resources available to assist individuals in permanently quitting smoking, such as a wide array of self-help materials and professional counseling services.

The provision of telephonic programs or counseling services, available during evenings and weekends, represents an accessible and efficacious approach for aiding individuals in smoking cessation. Individuals making phone inquiries are connected with experienced and proficient counselors who provide assistance in devising tailored strategies for smoking cessation aligned with their individual smoking habits.

Various support groups tailored for individuals seeking to discontinue their habits can also prove notably beneficial. They provide an opportunity to connect with individuals who are dedicated to cessation efforts and striving for a tobacco-free lifestyle. Hospitals, wellness centers, and workplaces offer specialized programs and classes that are facilitated by trained professionals. Furthermore, individuals who are unable to physically attend group meetings may utilize online support systems as an alternative means of accessing assistance.

The assistance and encouragement of your acquaintances and relatives can also hold significant value and prove particularly beneficial in your endeavor to cease this habit. Inform them about your intentions and make an effort to allocate time with individuals who do not engage in smoking or have successfully quit smoking, as they will undoubtedly provide significant support for your aspirations.

"Realigning One's Course of Action

A relapse does not indicate failure; rather, it is a common occurrence, particularly in cases of severe addiction. Many individuals have frequently given up on numerous occasions prior to attaining their objectives. When experiencing a relapse, it is advisable to reduce the quantity of cigarettes consumed. If your usual smoking consumption amounts to 10 cigarettes daily, limit it to just five during your relapse. Persevere, maintain optimism, and resist feelings of discouragement. Ceasing the activity can often require a substantial amount of time.

Stay Smoke-free

Maintaining steadfast dedication and remaining tobacco-free is regarded as the ultimate and pivotal aspect of the cessation journey. When you encounter the urge to smoke, recollect the initial reasons that compelled you to make the decision of quitting. Consider the numerous benefits it can bestow upon you and those in your social sphere.

Avoid drinking alcohol. If you are concerned about potential weight gain, it is advisable to develop a well-balanced dietary plan and establish a consistent exercise regimen to maintain your physical fitness.

Reward Yourself

Ceasing the habit of smoking may prove to be a formidable challenge for certain individuals; hence, it is recommended to commemorate one's achievement by utilizing the funds that would otherwise have been expended on smoking. Purchase a novel musical compilation, attend a cinematic exhibit, indulge in the gastronomic delights at your preferred dining establishment, or partake in physical exercise at a fitness facility.

The initial few days may prove to be the most challenging. Do not succumb to the temptation of surrendering under any circumstances. Seek out individuals who do not engage in smoking and explore novel and enjoyable pastimes in their company. Adopting a smoke-free lifestyle can yield numerous advantages, encompassing heightened vitality, improved financial prospects, enhanced physical appearance, and an extended lifespan with improved overall well-being.

www.ingramcontent.com/pod-product-compliance
Lightning Source LLC
Chambersburg PA
CBHW050417120526
44590CB00015B/1994